AN

ADDRESS

DELIVERED AT CAMBRIDGE

BEFORE THE SOCIETY OF THE

PHI BETA KAPPA,

26 JUNE, 1873.

BY

CHARLES FRANCIS ADAMS.

CAMBRIDGE:
PRESS OF JOHN WILSON AND SON.
1873.

AN

ADDRESS

DELIVERED AT CAMBRIDGE

BEFORE THE SOCIETY OF THE

PHI BETA KAPPA,

26 JUNE, 1873.

BY

CHARLES FRANCIS ADAMS.

CAMBRIDGE:
PRESS OF JOHN WILSON AND SON.
1873.

ADDRESS.

Mr. President and Gentlemen: —

I find a little difficulty in justifying to myself the rashness of accepting the invitation, with which I have been honored, to address you. It looks too much as if, in the face of so many admirable things done here by the ablest of our fraternity, chosen out of three successive generations of graduates, I were assuming that they had still left some part of their work for me to perfect. Moreover, I feel as if I were presenting myself in the position of a living anachronism of at least thirty years. The velocity with which the civilized world has moved in that time would seem to supply matter demanding the application of fresher and more flexible minds. A veteran laying down his armor for repose may indeed fight his battles over again for his own amusement, but he will scarcely pretend that he wields the vigor of the youth who is buckling for the fray. He may, indeed, delude himself and imagine that from the results of experience he has gathered some general conclusions not wholly inappropriate to the consideration of those who are to come after him. It is in this sense, and this only, that I have mustered courage to lay before you some poor thoughts on this our anniversary.

Possibly it should be added that not I alone, but even our Society too, bears marks of age, by reason whereof more than hints were uttered awhile ago that its mission had become too narrow to meet the demands of the expanding progeny of the University. Disclaiming any wish to assume intellectual refinement as the exclusive property of a class, it may yet be fairly argued in favor of select association in any pursuit that it is, after all, practically much the most effective stimulant to excellence. But, leaving the determination of that point, it may not be wholly out of place to glance for a moment at what our mission really has been, and how far it has attained a useful end.

It now lacks but little of a hundred years since its organization. Its object was the establishment of a bond of sympathy between the youthful students in American colleges in pursuit of the higher objects of education. It was a spontaneous impulse, premonitory of the widening nature of the demand about to be made upon their powers, and the resulting duty of increased preparation for the emergency. The manner of proceeding appears to have been simple enough. I have gained a tolerably clear view of the intent, from the possession of a diary kept by one of the early members, which has fallen into my hands. It was only four years after the Society was formed at this College that I find the following entry made in this book: —

> 21st June, 1786. "In the afternoon I was admitted, with Burge and Cranch, to the *Φ Β Κ* Society. It is established to promote friendship and literature in several of the universities of America."

It thus appears that a union was contemplated of a wider kind than had existed before among the youthful aspirants to advanced knowledge on this continent. The prosecution of a specific line of exercises seems to have been at that time contemplated. By this diary it would appear that certain under-graduates, selected from the Senior and Junior classes, were in the habit of assembling once a fortnight at the room of each member in his turn, to listen to a literary performance assigned to particular persons for that day. To illustrate this, I take from the same diary the following entries: —

29th August, 1786. "After prayer we had a meeting of the *Φ B K* at Freeman and Little's chamber. Mr. Ware presided, in the absence of Mr. Paine. Freeman read a short dissertation upon the love of our neighbor; Little and Packard, a forensic on the question whether the present scarcity of money in the Commonwealth be advantageous to it; Harris and Andrews, the extemporaneous disputants."

Whether in this discussion the disputants had had recourse to the essay of the founder of political economy in England, Adam Smith, published ten years before, does not appear. The fact is certain that at that moment no topic could be more interesting, for it was a time of great financial distress.

One fortnight later, the following record appears: —

12th September, 1786. "We had a meeting of the *Φ B K* at Burge's chamber. Bridge and Abbott read a forensic on the question whether internal tranquillity be proof of prosperity in a republic; Freeman and I, the extemporaneous disputants."

29th November, 1786. "Last night the *Φ B K* met at Burge's chamber. Little and Cranch read dissertations; Freeman and Packard, a disputation, whether 'Good order is promoted more by the rewarding of virtue than by the punishment of vice.' Mr. Ware and Mr. Harris disputed extempore."

From these extracts it is made to appear plainly enough that at this period the object of the association was to supplement the ordinary course of college training with a voluntary series of exercises in dialectics. To that end these youths occupied themselves, each in his turn, in the art of treating questions of public interest in two separate ways: the first, that of written argument, the offspring of study and research; the second, that of extemporaneous disputation, depending for its force upon the discipline acquired only by practice in drawing upon the mind at once. That there was growing a need of this kind of preparation for active life, seems clear enough; for the moment was critical enough outside of the college walls. Whilst these youths were discussing the way in which good order was to be promoted, there was any amount of disorder prevailing almost within a stone's throw, and threatening the very foundations of society. In this same diary, two days prior to the discussion, is the following entry:—

"This evening, just before prayers, about forty horsemen arrived here, under the command of Judge Prescott, of Groton, in order to protect the court to-morrow from the rioters. We hear of nothing but Shays and Shattuck. Two of the most despicable characters in the community now make themselves of great consequence."

The day after the discussion the record runs thus:—

"The weather very cold. No appearance of rioters as yet, though it is this evening reported that there are fifteen hundred within four miles of Cambridge."

Notwithstanding this menacing appearance, we are told that on the same evening the young men proceeded to have a dance at Chandler's chamber, just as if nothing was the matter.

But there never was in Massachusetts more just cause for alarm. The old colonial form of government established by an external authority had been swept away, and in its place had been substituted a new one, deriving its entire support from the consent of the people. And here was a very considerable portion of that people busily engaged in shaking the foundations upon which it rested by the application of physical force to prevent the administration of justice. Neither was the period much less critical for the College itself. It had from its origin closely entwined itself around the colonization of Massachusetts, and had made that process itself exceptional in history. As a general rule, the policy prompted by the discovery of America had led to the establishment, by the various powers of Europe, of dependencies all over the world, to be maintained only for their own pecuniary advantage. As a consequence, no observer can fail to perceive how little most of them have contributed during two centuries or more either to the moral, the social, or the literary improvement of mankind. It would seem as if the mere fact of a colonial condition were sure to entail upon every such community much the same species of subjection which ordinarily appertains to infancy in a family. Neither does this species of subordination quickly wear off. Let us for a moment look over the surface of the globe and notice how very small a proportion of the vast regions which have felt the stamp of European colonial enterprise has contributed any considerable share to the higher purposes of man. The ready way to account for this deficiency is by the fact that much the greatest part of these acquisitions has been treated solely as material for commercial speculation, the profits of which were to be gathered with little regard to any benefit other than the accumulation of wealth at home. Hence, no doubt, has come that habitual sense of vassalage, materially conflicting with a just sense of man's true destiny.

The condition of Massachusetts as it stood at the close of the war of independence had been made an exception to the general rule, simply for the reason that it never was, nor could have been, colonized for any similar purpose. It could have contributed few material resources to the mother country, plainly because its natural advantages yielded no proportion whatever to those which might be found more tempting elsewhere. Neither would Boston have derived from ordinary adventurers any position much above that of a third-rate fishing town. The root of its enduring vigor is found only in the moral resolution in which it started. Massachusetts would have been a cipher without the foundation of religious persecution upon which it was laid; neither could Boston have become the place it now is, without the foundation of religious and political education upon which this college of Cambridge was placed simultaneously with the settlement.

But I may be asked how I maintain my proposition that the College made the State and not the State the College. To which my answer is simple: that without the religious motive it would have been no object to men of the character of the first settlers to establish a political status here, or even to come at all; and, with that motive, political and moral instruction was an indispensable instrument to the successful prosecution of the religious enterprise. The result was that a college must be established for the purpose of insuring a succession of scholars who should be able to uphold the peculiar combination of policy in Church and State which they had it at heart to perpetuate.

Thus it happened that the maintenance of education, though an incidental rather than a direct consequence of this policy, secured through the theological conflict of the hour, and its perpetual appeal to the authority of the Scriptures, the presence of a reading population for the moment, and simultaneously the necessary provision to continue it, a self-directing community, for the future.

But if Massachusetts enjoys the peculiar honor in the history of colonization of making education coeval with its origin, it does not necessarily follow that the process would be carried on with vigor after the disappearance of the founders. On the contrary, experience teaches the danger of a retrograde tendency in succeeding generations not sustained by equally strong convictions. It is comparatively an easy work to found a college. That of perpetuating it in the face of a decaying popular sympathy is the great labor. In order to counteract this, new motives must be supplied and a continuity of interest preserved. The colonial records furnish a sufficient explanation of how this came about. Where freedom of discussion is permitted, differences of opinion are inevitable. And upon the gravest questions affecting man's future condition, founded on opposing constructions of Holy Writ, expression of sentiment becomes a duty. Hence the interest taken in controversy.

It is, then, the spirit of religious controversy maintained during the second generation, which contributed the means of keeping up the popular interest in this College. Controversy necessarily implies the possession of certain gifts, most readily made effective by culture in a university. It is invigorated by access to the higher sources of learning and the discipline imposed by the study of logic. Moreover, the sense of opposition rouses an energy which stamps force on the language giving expression to thought. So likewise, the very fact of controversy, especially on the most momentous of questions, touching equally the interests of all human kind, engages the sympathies on the opposing sides, even of the most sluggish. No more striking evidence of this truth remains than the brilliant triumphs of Blaise Pascal, who by the pure force of his logic and his wit enlisted even the frivolous and volatile of his countrymen in the study of the most abstruse polemics, carried on by him under the pseudonym of Louis de Montalte, to expose the fallacies of the strongest of the Roman Catholic orders.

Hence it may, I think, be safely affirmed, from this review of the first century of the colonial period, that its political and literary life was sustained by the presence of Harvard College, from whose portals issued many sons, at least one half of them devoted to the work of promoting the religious culture of the people. At this day, if we look back upon the details of what appears to us wearisome and unprofitable contention, we are apt to wonder how it was possible that it should have held its interest so long. The fact that it did so, and thereby entailed a blessing, however indirect, is enough for us. It preserved the College through its most critical period. For it may be readily assumed that there is nothing great institutions of learning have more to dread in the loss of influence than a passive or sluggish reception by the community of the lessons it is their province to disseminate.

The interest thus maintained in the preservation of an elevated standard of scholarship throughout the critical period of colonial infancy had another good effect, apart from the agitation of solemn questions of welfare hereafter. It incidentally furnished the means of checking in another manner the retrograde tendency almost inseparable from new and isolated communities in the generations immediately succeeding that of the founders. It was the presence of the College which supplied the means of practically executing the legal provisions for the primary forms of instruction generally. Experience long ago taught the danger of leaving these to degenerate in the hands of ignorant pretenders. It has often happened to a small community, starting with quiet self-complacency, on a conviction that its system of teaching was the best in the world, to be, after an interval more or less long, rudely forced to open its eyes to the fact that pedantic and pretentious ignorance had become nestled in the garb intended for scholarship and skill. Nothing makes rust so fast as routine. The maxim so trite among us that the price of liberty is eternal vigilance is not less true as applied to all sorts of proficiency in learning.

Thus passed the ecclesiastical period of our educational history. It served its turn to protect the infancy and growth of colonial society, and on the whole it did it well. But the time came when another and very different species of contention called for a new species of preparation. The newspaper press began to take the place of the pulpit, and secular antagonists appeared more prominently in the arena. But it soon appeared that, however different the persons, the arms used in the new warfare had been welded in the same forge. Quite a century has passed away since this species of literary progress took its place in our history, soon to be forgotten like its predecessor. It fell to my lot some years since to look up more or less of it; and from a perusal I think I may safely say that, considering the relative size of this community and its colonial dependence, nothing more strikingly illustrates the blessed influence of the spirit infused into the people by the education given at Cambridge than the masterly manner in which difficult problems of law and government were handled by those who had received their instruction only from that source.

The political revolution which established the State as a component part of an independent nation effected a change not less abrupt in the condition of the College. Its identity with the religious movement of the age began to fade, and, in lieu of it, appeared a more exclusive devotion to literature and science. For the first time in history, intellectual culture was recognized and enjoined in terms as a constituent portion of the organic system of government matured for the people of a new political State, and it was expressly made the duty of all public officers to cherish all institutions of learning generally; and "ESPECIALLY THE UNIVERSITY AT CAMBRIDGE."

How far that injunction has been practically carried out during the ninety years that have since elapsed it is no part of my present purpose to discuss. If a smaller proportion of material assistance has been supplied than might have been reasonably expected, any deficiency has been fully made up from the spontaneous munificence of individual citizens. I think I said, a little while ago, that the city of Boston owed its present position, in a measure, to the benefits received from the proximity of this College. If so, I may confidently say to her honor that never was the obligation of gratitude more lavishly redeemed by her sons, and that too by many who never received any advantage from the instruction, but who were prompted by an instinctive and a just conviction that the charges so solemnly laid upon them in the fundamental act of the social system were wise and good, and they were prepared to abide by them, whoever else might fail.

Coeval with the adoption of the State Constitution was the impulse to organize new methods for the promotion of science. Hence sprang up associations incorporated to that end, and others which have been maintained with success by purely voluntary labors, down to this day. Among the number is to be reckoned the literary society, the members of which I have now the honor to address. It is not an uninteresting fact, illustrative of the great change then taking place in our whole social system, that it did not derive its origin from within our own borders. It came from a spot whence, of all others, we should least expect it, the College of William and Mary, in the colony of Virginia. What it was that prompted the youthful students there to make nearly simultaneous overtures to those of all other colleges then known in America, for the establishment of affiliated societies for self-improvement in literature and philosophy, does not clearly appear. However that may be, it seemed the dawn of a new era, when institutions of learning on this continent first determined to overstep the narrow limits of colonial authority, and look broadly over the land. Not the least singular circumstance attending it was that the project was carried on with the most industry precisely at the most critical period of the war, and at moments when the fortune of the struggling colonies of the South seemed at its lowest ebb. Concurrently with the first meeting held here, Lord Cornwallis was making his way over all opposition in North Carolina toward the very point in Virginia from whence the instigation first came. Yet there seems to have been no relaxation of these pursuits so much more congenial with times of peace. Very surely it would have been a vast advance, had the plan embraced any forms of co-operation; but that object does not appear ever to have been contemplated. Even the original and useful exercises first adopted here, as already described, have been long since laid aside. Instead of improving the young and the ambitious at their start in life, the practice has since been to celebrate a single day as an anniversary, and, after the Roman example in war, to raise some old *evocatus* like myself to inculcate precepts more eagerly caught from younger lips.

The decline of religious and political controversy very naturally followed the establishment of all the constituent elements of a nation on a peaceful foundation. Hence it has happened that during the greater part of the present century the cause of education here has ceased to be connected with the casual agitations of the outer world, and has been more exclusively directed to improvement in literary and moral and scientific pursuits in the abstract. This has, on the whole, been a wise course, though attended by the disadvantage of diminishing the general interest of the country in what is done. Yet, on looking back on what the College has to show for itself, it is not unreasonable to claim for it the merit of having introduced to a constantly expanding theatre of public action a very fair share of the men who, in all the highest occupations of life, have acquitted themselves with honor to it and to themselves,—learned divines, eminent statesmen, profound lawyers and legislators, eloquent orators, qualified writers in science and literature and history, whose works will be their monument. In brief, the College can fairly claim that it has fulfilled its mission to an extent to earn for it the respect and gratitude of the country.

At the same time that I admit this merit for the past, it is no more than fair to allow that the period did not elapse without leaving traces of our painful transition from a colonial to an independent condition, as well in matters of literature and learning as in government. It is not to be denied that a degree of implicit deference for a while habitual in the more educated class, not solely to the forms of instruction, but to the dicta of the writers in the mother country, remained to depress our native energy and to check the development of original thought. Long after the establishment of our political status the symptoms of this species of vassalage continued to appear. Neither were we without the benefit of occasional reminders of it from the parent State. How many years is it since one of her supercilious magazine writers asked the question, "Who reads an American book?" Neither was it, at that time, easy to deny some justice to the taunt. The writer, doubtless, overlooked the fact that the same question might have been asked in his own country, with no better answer any time for nearly five hundred years before the appearance of Chaucer. There as here, intellectual dependence has been more or less a consequence of the revival of learning in the Middle Ages. What would have been the condition of human civilization at this moment, if we had waited for original genius to develop it in Great Britain or anywhere else in the northern region of Europe? The light which blazed on it sprang from a narrow belt on the globe's surface, stretching along the eastern semicircle of the Mediterranean Sea. To that quarter, and to that alone, can we look for the sources of all the religion, all the law, all the philosophy, and all the literature which has distinguished the civilization of modern times everywhere. Unhappy will be the day when we shall throw off that dependence, or cease to encourage the most intimate access to those precious stores of intellectual and moral and religious culture which have thus far contributed so much to elevate the condition of man.

For the rest, the progress made of late years in literary authorship puts completely to flight all these assumptions of degeneracy. Yet I am not of those optimists who imagine that nothing remains to be done to secure excellence in our modes of education. On the contrary, I somewhat apprehend that over the whole extent of the land, taken as one surface, sciolism is becoming the rule and the proportion of ignorance multiplies rather than diminishes. Rapidly as the number of scholars has of late advanced in the best endowed Universities, it seems to me to bear no adequate relation to the increasing demand of the times and the growth of the population. Am I extravagant if I estimate the proper proportion of scholars who should be fitting themselves for the great work, at this University alone, at not less than ten thousand? In order to meet the exigencies of the times, there should spring up an enthusiasm for learning such as of yore burst forth in the great institutions of Europe. Quite six centuries ago, when Great Britain had nothing like its present aggregate of population, and even that now falls below ours, it is affirmed in the books that at Oxford there were not less at one time than thirty thousand scholars. At the University in Paris at about the same time there were twenty-five thousand. At Bologna, the students of law alone numbered ten thousand. Conceding any measure of exaggeration in these figures, the fact of the existence of this enthusiasm is attested beyond reasonable dispute. And we can only explain it by assuming a degree of zeal in the youthful generation of that day, which is the condition precedent of all true national advancement anywhere.

I believe the great want of the time among us in America is a little more of this enthusiasm. We are apt to measure education not so much by its excellence as by its price. Hence the multitude of minor institutions spread abroad over the country, which are doubtless good as far as they go, but they cannot go very far. At such places enthusiasm becomes difficult, if not impossible. If lighted at all, the fire must be spread by the teacher among numbers working together. In the days of my youth at this University I cannot disguise my impression that the method was formal, mechanical, and cold. No scholar dreamed of sympathy with him in his difficulties, or regarded his exercise otherwise than as a task, for the failure to perform which he lost credit, or at best won a step over his comrades by success. In either event the teacher looked like Minos or Rhadamanthus. In my mind the true maxim is the old one of Horace, applicable as freely to instruction as to the drama: —

> "Si vis me flere, dolendum est
> Primum ipsi tibi."

A mighty loadstone is human sympathy! I say this not with any design to reflect on the absence of it in the mode of instruction pursued at this day, but rather with a conviction that a great change has been going on since my time, which only needs expansion to supersede all that may remain of the old habits.

I now come to one subject which may possibly be somewhat new to treat of in this presence, yet which I cannot but think most important in connection with the progress of American education. It seems to me there is a want which ought before long to be supplied everywhere and especially here. I refer to the arrangement of a class of preliminary studies especially adapted to the preparation of young men, to take an efficient part in the treatment of difficult questions connected with the management of public affairs. It is not denied that the roll of the University bears the names of many graduates who have served their country with honor to her and to themselves, under various circumstances of grave responsibility. But even these examples appear to me, generally, to prove that the training, which they acquired by slow degrees in after life, often incidentally in connection with a profession not always calculated to secure the best or the most complete results, might be much more effectively commenced here, and prosecuted independently afterwards. There are many ambitious young men all over the country, and the number grows every year, who need and who would grace just such an occupation.

It has indeed been often urged as an objection to this course that, however the case might be elsewhere, there is no dependence to be placed in America upon public life as a career. Where the sole reliance must be upon popular favor, the means to which persons are compelled to resort in order to secure it are often so repulsive that no man of nice sensibility can long submit to use them without self-degradation. Besides which, even under the most favorable aspect of circumstances, there is a liability incurred of sacrificing more or less of honest convictions to the dictatorial spirit of party, which cannot fail, sooner or later, to undermine the spirit of independence. It is objected to me that experience proves the greater portion of the people to prefer a superficial pretender, who has learned nothing but the art of ingratiating himself, to any man of superior accomplishment and elevated character, who knows no disguises and scorns making bargains. Hence I have often heard it maintained that one of the results of our present system of Government is, in a measure, the exclusion from public life of the highest talent and character, and the substitution of a class of persons little fitted for great responsibility, either by capacity, acquirement, or morals, and possessing only an acuteness, improved by long-continued practice, to scent out the popular inclination of the hour, and so to shape their conduct as to secure the best chance of benefit from it to themselves. Thus it is concluded by some that a steady tendency to degenerate is so perceptible in the administration of public affairs that it is not worth the while of any young man who aspires to a high standard of excellence to think of venturing in so desperate a pursuit.

I have listened often to much of just this sort of reasoning, but, I frankly confess, with a very slight inclination to yield to its soundness. If the effect be, as it is alleged, the existence of a considerable amount of reserved power, now lying dormant in the country, because excluded from all opportunity of a career by these alleged causes, all that I can say in reply is, that, if fault there be, it must lie with those who decline to develop their qualities more palpably to the public eye, rather than with the community at large for not properly appreciating them. There is such a thing as being so fastidious about means as never to be able to reach a practical end. There may likewise be a form of constitutional sluggishness which covers an aversion to the labors and obligations incident to successful exertion under the guise of want of opportunity. My own conviction always has been and still is, that under no system of government now known is there more full and free opportunity given to all, in whatever condition of life, usefully to develop every natural or acquired power they may possess, as in none is there a more ready inclination on the part of the public to appreciate both services and character. And, if this proposition be admitted, then I should say, still further, that in no place should the means for developing such powers be more abundantly supplied than in our Universities of the highest class.

In saying what I have, let me not be misunderstood. If the purpose of this laborious preparation be merely a desire to obtain this or that high official position in the State, then will the pursuit doubtless be attended with more or less severe disappointment. Success or failure in reaching definite objects in life, we all know, depends upon such an infinite variety of contingencies wholly beyond our control, that no man is wise in risking his hopes of usefulness upon any narrow chance of fortune.

I should feel myself to be very much belittling the recommendation I venture to make to my young friends to cultivate a taste for statesmanship of the widest scope, if I were to associate it in general with the hope of getting into power. Nor yet do I mean to go so far as to underrate that object, considered as a means of developing innate force to purposes of good. I quite concur in the wisdom of Lord Bacon, when he says that "such power is the true and lawful end of aspiring; for good thoughts, though God accept them, yet towards men are little better than good dreams, except they be put in act; and that cannot be without power and place as the vantage and commanding ground." I should, however, venture to question the exclusive feature of the condition. I agree that power and place are "vantage and commanding ground," but I would go no farther. On the contrary, it has for some time past appeared to me to be one of the wants of the time and the country, that of a class of persons bred in our largest institutions of learning, fitted to be exponents of doctrine in the science of

Government and of natural and international law, though with a very secondary view to the casual acquisition of place. If not themselves possessing that commanding ground, they are at any rate in a condition to enlighten those who do, in cases when some of them, at least, appear to stand in great need of it. I say, then, that what is most wanted is honest, independent opinion, founded upon extensive study and superior knowledge, and not likely to be warped by incidental temptations of this or that brief elevation to a public post, or to follow the *ignis fatuus* of personal ambition until it plunges the wanderer irretrievably into a morass. Hence high place may indeed be desired as a means of usefulness; but as a warning of the ruinous effect of it on the possessor when carried too far, no instance illustrates it better than that of Lord Bacon himself.

It should be kept in mind that in considering this subject I put wholly out of view any association with the ordinary party politics of the country as wholly foreign from the proper neutrality of a great seat of education. In the prosecution of the study of the science of Government in all its various ramifications, there is not the smallest occasion to mingle with it an interest in the casual struggles of the hour. The preparation for action which I should desire would have in view chiefly two fields of usefulness to the nation, in due proportion to its rapid expansion over space. One of these is in the direction of the Periodical Press. The other is in that of public speaking with effect.

When I compare the state of the Newspaper Press as it is now with what it was at the commencement of the Federal government, it seems to me that of all the changes that have taken place in our social system this is the most striking. Then a semi-weekly, or possibly a daily journal, in the largest towns, was conducted for the most part by a laboring printer, who confined himself to the task of filling his sheet with news casually picked up, and relied for the treatment of topics of momentary interest upon such voluntary contributions as could be secured from promising young men, amply paid by seeing their productions in print. Now and then a heavier pen would endeavor to enlighten the community on a grave and important subject. But the circle of readers would be at best very limited, unless in a few cases where republication might be thought an object in the few large towns. It was in this way that Hamilton and Madison and Jay labored and succeeded, not without serious difficulty, in disseminating the views which effected the adoption of the Constitution. But although a few able writers might gain admission to several presses which could unitedly operate upon opinion in some cases, it by no means followed that access would be given even to the strongest pen which should venture to reason, however forcibly, against any earnest popular excitement. The loss of some subscribers might ensue, and that loss would be enough to cripple the paper. The party lines, too, were closely drawn, so that no person disposed to express an independent sentiment of a controversial nature could rely upon a hearing. The cry of "Stop my paper!" was too frequent and too formidable not to inspire great caution in touching angry questions. The effect was a practical exclusion of independent thought, and the multiplication of presses which studied rather to follow in the wake of public opinion than to lead it.

We have outgrown all this. And the new condition, though not unattended with evils of its own, must be admitted to be far in advance of the old one. Many presses now spread their circulation so far and wide that they no longer have reason to dread the consequences of maintaining a free, unbiassed course. Party organs, purely as such, rather lose than gain a foothold with considerable numbers. And in the treatment of questions of great interest there is rapidly growing up a demand upon the most competent sources, of whatever they may be pleased to furnish, without calling the sentiment in question. The mere name of a writer of established weight is sufficient to secure him free admittance somewhere or other to the public view. Nay, the thing has gone farther than this in Europe, and even in some places in America. Persons believed to be the best qualified to treat some particular subject, for the moment exciting an interest, are eagerly sought for, and liberal compensation offered for their work, if desired. The effect of this must naturally be to present additional inducements to the cultivation of the particular gifts which secure similar results. One consequence has actually been, in the chief countries of Europe, a mode of treating the higher questions of morals and politics, law and government, by the public press, very much in advance of the practice of ancient times.

And just so must it be with us presently, if not now. The effect ought to be to raise up a class of persons fitted to meet the particular want. How much that want was felt during the critical portion of the late war may well be measured by the painful monuments of error which remain as a warning on the records of the legislative department of the government. The rudiments of an education of such a class should be taught at this University. They will stand in no need of place to benefit the public, and yet they will be fitted for it if called on any suitable emergency. In any event, they will be likely to guide public opinion without regard to personal considerations. Such men make the best of advisers. I may be permitted to cite an example that occurs to me as a fine illustration of my meaning. I would respectfully point to the learned treatment by the venerable person lately the President of the University at New Haven, our foremost rival in good works, of the chief disputed questions growing out of the last treaty with Great Britain. Free as he is from all possible ambition for place, he has yet been doing a service to us and the world in general, for which the nation should count him one of its benefactors.

For the reasons thus stated, I have been led to believe that a wide field is open for an honorable career, in the treatment, with adequate knowledge, of great questions in history, laws, and government, through the opening furnished by the public press, independent of any prospect of advancement in public life. The foundation of learning in this career should be laid at the University, and the chief instruments to gain complete success must be the power to write with knowledge, with clearness, and with force.

But this is not the only opening to distinction, without primary regard to place. In every form of popular government, the greatest source of personal reputation, as well as of public usefulness, has always been, and in my opinion will always be, the gift of eloquence. I do not propose to define by this term the mere faculty, not uncommon among us, of expressing our thoughts with facility and grace. My conditions rise much higher, to the sources which must be provided beforehand. The subject has been so admirably treated by Cicero, that any detail here would be superfluous. But Cicero did not have to learn in his day a thousandth part of what must be known now to complete the substance of an accomplished speaker. The single department of history alone, not to speak of law and literature and science, furnishes a rich mine of illustration, which can be worked for years with great profit. Of this the ancients had comparatively little. How small a state was Athens! And how few topics had even Demosthenes to handle in dealing with a single enemy, however powerful, abroad, and a handful of rivals at home! Even the far wider grasp of Cicero could not spread beyond the confines of the republic and its tributaries, however broad that space might then appear. How infinitely expanded is the field at this time, when all the great nations of the globe are within hearing of one another! An orator in the British House of Commons or the French Assembly will at almost the same moment fix the attention of his rival contemporaries in St. Petersburg and Washington, in Pekin and Constantinople. It may be said that the claim advanced so ridiculously by Anacharsis Cloots in the great overturn in France, of being the orator of the human race, is becoming more and more susceptible of realization by some really gifted person who may appear as time goes on. But I should weary your patience, were I to attempt to tell how many elements seem to me essential to the production of such a man. With these in his possession, no power short of physical constraint could suppress his influence. The records of civilization transmit to us only here and there a name associated with great triumphs of this power, and still more rarely the evidence upon which the reputation rested. A single Greek and a single Roman have become identified with our conceptions of the greatest excellence in this art. But the same path has not been untrodden since, and with a greater or less share of that fame which never dies. I conscientiously believe that this gift, in its highest state of perfection, can be made the greatest moral instrument of good vouchsafed to man by the Creator. Why, then, shall it not be cultivated, with little reference to mere aspirations of ordinary ambition? Who is there who would not rather envy the powers of Demosthenes than those of Alexander of Macedon? Who would not prefer the triumphs of Cicero to those of Augustus? Both of them died by violence, it is true. But was not that violence the most indisputable testimony possible to be paid to their superiority?

Hence I respectfully submit the question to my brethren, whether it be not alike a dictate of prudence and a precept of patriotism to urge the establishment here of the best possible system for bringing forward aspiring youth adequately to grapple with the momentous and ever-expanding problems presented by the social and political movements of the time? Admitting that the requisite training cannot be completed during the brief period assigned for study here, at least it can be commenced, and a distinct practical road marked out to follow afterwards. I find nothing of the kind existing here at present. The idea seems to prevail that an orator, like a poet, is born, not made, whilst the fact is clear that a real orator is the most artificial product of human education. Not more so is the splendid pile of St. Peter's at Rome. Yet if it be pleaded that in this relatively old and well-endowed institution the means are not at command to provide young aspirants at once with all they need to develop powers to fulfil with credit the very highest duties of life, I know not where, in the broad domain of the republic, they can hope for such facilities. We must be content with mediocrity for ever. We cannot even hope to provide for the secondary duty of counteracting the pestilent effects of the specious sophistry of the half-fledged demagogues of the hour, by perfecting more exalted models, both able and willing to contribute their full share to prove what it is truly to constitute a State. Late events seem to have shown, in a manner not to be misunderstood, that very many persons at present occupying high public trusts have erred most painfully, not so much from evil intent as from the absence of that which high education supplies, a nice sense of moral discrimination in public conduct. But there is even a wider scope for the exercise of a wholesome influence over opinion in the community at large, which would soon make similar offences impossible.

Let us not despair of a remedy. The times are critical, not here alone, but all over the world. Prospering in purely material interests, as I fully believe the people at large have never done before, the elements to bring on the gravest moral changes are simultaneously at work everywhere. The problems now lavishly presented for agitation touch the very foundations of religious faith, of moral philosophy, of civil government, and even of human society. New forms of power are developing themselves, seriously menacing the solidity of all established institutions. Even that great conviction ever cherished as the apple of our eye, and which really is the rock upon which our political edifice rests, the durability of representative government, bids fair to be sooner or later drawn into question on solid grounds. The collision between the forces of associated capital and those of associated labor is likely to make itself felt throughout all the wide extent of human civilization. Much as we unquestionably advance in education, in refinement, and in the spread of the blessed spirit of benevolence, some fearful catastrophe now and then, on a sudden, opens our minds to horrors of a bestial ferocity still clinging to the animal nature, which would have disgraced the rudest age of the creation. Hence it seems difficult to deny that we make almost even progress in our philanthropy and in the magnitude of our crimes.

If it be conceded that this is so, and that the elements of good and evil are yet gathering with almost equal energy to try their strength in a conflict, so much the more imperative becomes the duty of those who aspire to the glory of promoting noble objects to waste no opportunities of fortifying their powers for the fray, — so much the more imperative is it upon the highest institutions in this land, the great arsenals of supply, to furnish every kind of armor with which the more certainly an ultimate triumph of the right and the true may be secured.

Cast a momentary glance over the surface of this broad continent. You will see at once that it is the most magnificent theatre upon which human power has ever had an opportunity to exert itself. Remember that upon it forty millions of beings are already placed, and that the future will doubtless contribute its annual millions in an ever-increasing ratio. You will also note that, flocking in from abroad, come the Celt, the Teuton, the African, the Aztec, and the native of far Cathay; all rushing in to form parts of one huge conglomerate mass of restless humanity, upon whose fiat depends the realization of the highest hopes ever yet formed of approaching the image of a Utopian commonwealth. Surely never in any preceding record of human history has there been a fairer opening for the full development of the noblest aspirations for good, which the Divine Being has been pleased to implant in the bosoms of His creatures. Here is ample space and verge enough for the most far-seeing statesman, the most persuasive orator, the most profound philosopher, the most exalted philanthropist. Here is a field the like of which Aristotle or Plato never trod. Here are problems on which Cicero never could have speculated, or Bacon exercised his wonderful sagacity. Answer me, if you can, I pray you, shall it indeed be that this marvellous scene will be occupied by actors worthy of their place, who will strain their utmost powers to rise to every great emergency, and do for their fellow-men all that mortal power has been able to effect, since the forfeiture of Paradise?

Let us hope that the enthusiasm for a higher education

may and will stimulate the young to weave for themselves a garland of laurels, wherefrom they may spread over their brows an everlasting crown; and out of them the historian shall mark the good, the wise, the true, for lessons to the multitude unborn.

Blessed, indeed, will be the Alma Mater who shall be able to cry out, "These are my sons." Sad will be her reproach if she should find them emanate from any inferior source!

www.ingramcontent.com/pod-product-compliance
Lightning Source LLC
LaVergne TN
LVHW011627120826
845150LV00012B/2350

* 9 7 8 1 4 1 8 1 9 4 2 9 1 *